THE INSIDE-OUTSIDE
BOOK OF PARIS
ROXIE MUNRO

PAVILION BOOKS LIMITED   LONDON

First published in Great Britain in 1992 by PAVILION BOOKS LIMITED
196 Shaftesbury Avenue, London WC2H 8JL

Text and illustrations copyright © Roxie Munro 1992

Designed by Joseph Rutt

A CIP catalogue record for this book is available from the British Library.

Printed and bound in Hong Kong by South China Printing Co.

ISBN 1 85145 749 6   10 9 8 7 6 5 4 3 2 1

To Bo, because it's Paris

Acknowledgements
Thanks to Donna Brooks, my editor; Bo Zaunders, for his
help with research; Karen Lotz; Joseph Rutt, for book
design; and in Paris, JoAnne Morning.

Musée d'Orsay

The enormous vaulted space of
the Orsay Museum was originally
a railway station. Built of glass
and steel in 1900, it has now
been turned into one of the most
popular museums in Paris,
specializing in nineteenth-century
art. Over 600 people work
inside, greeting visitors and taking
care of the vast exhibits. Spanning
the years 1848 to 1914, the
Orsay collections feature many
Impressionist paintings as well
as sculpture, decorative arts,
photography and the very
earliest films.

Looking through one of the old railway clocks, visitors can gaze across the Seine, the river that winds through Paris, to the Tuileries Gardens and, on the right, a former palace of many French kings, now a great museum — the Louvre. During the height of the tourist season, more than 30,000 people a day may visit the Orsay Museum.

Booksellers along the Seine

Most days, depending upon the weather, sellers of old prints, maps, postcards and secondhand books do a brisk business from their zinc-topped book boxes along both banks of the Seine. Here browsers

enjoy the wares of a group of Left Bank booksellers, called
bouquinistes. In the background are the Pont St Michel (a bridge)
and buildings on the Ile de la Cité (an island in the Seine).

Nearby is Shakespeare and Company, a bookshop started in the 1920s by Sylvia Beach. Originally located on Rue de l'Odéon, it was a favourite haunt of writers like James Joyce, F. Scott Fitzgerald and Ernest Hemingway, who said he found books there that he had

never seen before. Now Shakespeare and Company has the largest
selection of English-language books on the continent of Europe.
On Sunday afternoons book-lovers can have tea and listen to
visiting authors talk about their books.

Jardin des Tuileries

Filled with statues of horses, nymphs and gods, the Tuileries is a perfect example of a French formal garden. It was created in 1664 on the site of a tile-works factory that left behind its French name, *tuileries*. Adjoining the section shown here is a vast expanse of trees planted in an orderly pattern. In 1783 one of the first hot-air balloons was launched here.

This lavishly decorated merry-go-round under the trees, called *La Belle Epoque Carrousel*, gives rides to children for a few francs. Its name, meaning 'The Good Old Days', refers to a period of elegance and gaiety that characterized Parisian life from the mid nineteenth century until World War I.

L'Arc de Triomphe

A small plane once flew through this majestic arch, built by Napoléon in the early 1800s to commemorate his army's victories. The Arch of Triumph, 164 feet high and 148 feet wide, stands imposingly at Place Charles de Gaulle, where twelve avenues converge. Beneath the arch an eternal flame marks the resting place of France's unknown soldier.

The view from the observation deck shows why the arch's location was originally called Place de l'Etoile (*étoile* means 'star' in French). To the left you can see the Champs-Elysées, the most famous avenue in Paris. Originally swampland, then a tree-lined promenade for carriages, it now draws throngs of tourists to its many cafés, shops and theatres.

Ecole des Beaux-Arts

Once a residence for monks and later a museum, the Ecole des Beaux-Arts was established in 1816 as an art school. Students share studio space but work independently, meeting privately with their professors for instruction and critique. The school is located in the Latin Quarter, home of the Sorbonne, a university founded in 1215, when the language in all places of learning was Latin.

Café la Palette, down the street from the Ecole des Beaux-Arts, is a favourite hangout for artists. Paris has over 12,000 cafés — gathering-places where people can drink coffee and gossip, exchange ideas, read, or just watch the world go by. Cafés have been an integral part of the city's cultural and social life for over 300 years.

The mural in the Bastille underground station commemorates the start
of the French Revolution, when mobs stormed the Bastille, a prison
and hated symbol of royal tyranny. The style of the Metro entrance

is art nouveau, in vogue in 1900, when the first line opened for the
Paris World Fair. One billion people a year now ride the attractive,
clean and — thanks to rubber wheels — quiet Paris underground.

Centre National d'Art Contemporain Georges Pompidou

Constructed in 1977, the bold, high-tech Pompidou Centre contains collections of modern art and industrial design as well as language labs, a bookshop and even a children's museum. The centre is also known as the Beaubourg, after the plateau on which it stands. On one side the building's network of exposed pipes, ducts and other fixtures reveal their functions through brightly painted colours: green for the water system, yellow for electrical circuits, blue for air-conditioning and red for escalators and lifts.

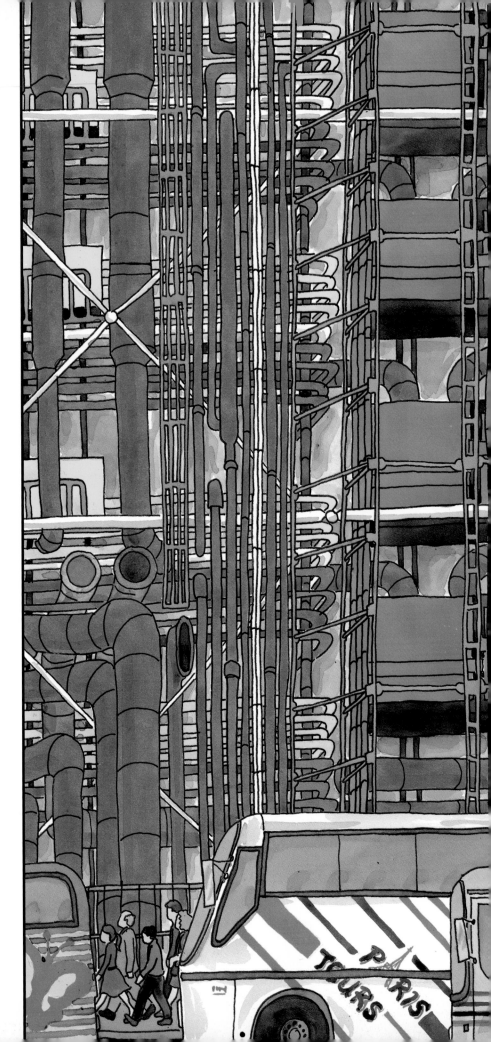

On the opposite side of the
building, dizzying, see-through
escalators offer a view across Paris
all the way to Montmartre and the
Basilica of the Sacred Heart, as
well as a glimpse down to the
street musicians, singers and
magicians performing in the
square below.

Les Bateaux Mouches

The *bateaux mouches* ('river steamers') travel under more than
two dozen of the thirty-two bridges that cross the Seine in Paris.
Originally these wide, flat boats offered Parisians cheap, convenient

transport, but now they primarily provide visitors with a leisurely open-air tour of the city.

The bridges of Paris are low because river traffic consists mainly
of barges. This single-span bridge, the ornate Pont Alexandre III,
built in 1900, is only twenty-five feet above the water. Many of

the old barges tied up along the quays have been converted to
floating homes.

Le Marché

Delicious fresh vegetables and fruits, poultry, fish, cheese, eggs and butter are just some of the reasons to visit an open-air market, or *marché*. This one on the Rue Mouffetard tempts Parisians, who like to buy their food fresh each day, with everything from live chickens to cherries. Throughout Paris there are special markets for things like flowers, birds and stamps, and there are also many flea and antique markets.

Shoppers may take home fresh baguettes of bread from the bakery, or *boulangerie*, as often as three times a day. This woman is going to her home in the Marais, one of the oldest districts of Paris, splendidly restored in recent times. Its twisting streets contain fine examples of seventeenth- and eighteenth-century mansions.

Appearance is just as important as taste where pastry is concerned.
Six basic doughs, whose recipes were developed centuries ago,
are the basis for all French pastries. Decorating with fruits, nuts,

chocolates and glazes is an art in itself. One French pastry chef of the early 1800s sought inspiration from museums and then made etchings that were copied in pastry.

Marionnettes

Inside a small wooden building under the shade of trees in the Champs-de-Mars, the park next to the Eiffel Tower, is a puppet theatre. It gives performances every Wednesday, Saturday and Sunday as well as on school holidays. Puppet shows are a favourite pastime of Parisian children. There are several other such theatres in Paris, including those in the Luxembourg Gardens and the Tuileries.

The beautifully costumed puppets (*marionnettes* in French) are made and operated by Luigi Tirelli, for whom being a puppeteer is a family tradition. These characters, from the French children's classic 'Le Trézor du Roy d'Agobert', are constructed of wood, fabric, paint and various decorative materials. Monsieur Tirelli also performs 'Cinderella' and other well-known children's stories.

Tour Eiffel (cover)

Called Gustave Eiffel's 'folly' and 'useless and monstrous' as it was being built, the Eiffel Tower is now without doubt the symbol of Paris. Erected for the 1889 Paris Universal Exposition, the tower was never meant to be permanent. But because the first transatlantic wireless telephones were operated from the tower, it endured. Composed of 12,000 iron pieces and 2.5 million rivets, this 1,051-foot-tall (including the antenna) structure took 300 steeplejacks two years to build. Like the staircases go diagonally up the legs. Novelties have ridden up the 1,792 steps, and an elephant once walked up them. In good weather the view from the top extends forty-five to fifty miles.

Cathédrale de Notre-Dame de Paris (opening pages)

The Cathedral of Our Lady of Paris stands on the Ile de la Cité, a small island in the Seine where Celtic fishermen called Parisii settled around 250 BC. Houses of worship have occupied the site for over 2,000 years. The cathedral, a perfect example of Gothic architecture, was begun in 1163 and took 182 years to build. In medieval times, the finely chiseled stone figures on the three portal facades were intended to provide a sort of sculptural Bible for the common folk who couldn't read. All distances from Paris are measured from kilomètre zéro — a brass compass-like star embedded in the pavement outside the west door. From this spot, visitors can look northeast to see where the Ile de la Cité, the River Seine, began over millenniums.

Fini